P9-DBT-459

# Katherine Dunham

# Katherine Dunham

## Pioneer of Black Dance

Barbara O'Connor

TRAILBLAZER
BIOGRAPHY

Carolrhoda Books, Inc./Minneapolis

*For my mom,*
*  with love*

Special thanks to Lark, Flip, Valerie, Doanne, Deanna, Delia, Debbie, Sue, Leslie, and Marshall—who listen with open minds—and speak with open hearts; to Janet, my pal and partner; Jill Anderson, for her fine editing (once again); Theodore Jamison of the Southern Illinois University East St. Louis Center for the Performing Arts; Damon Smith and Jeanelle Stovall of the Katherine Dunham Centers for the Arts and Humanities; Marie-Christine Dunham-Pratt; and, especially, Katherine Dunham for providing information for this book.

Text copyright © 2000 by Barbara O'Connor

Carolrhoda Books, Inc.
A Division of Lerner Publishing Group
241 First Avenue North
Minneapolis, MN 55401 U.S.A.

Website address: www.lernerbooks.com


Library of Congress Cataloging-in-Publication Data

O'Connor, Barbara.
   Katherine Dunham : pioneer of black dance / Barbara O'Connor.
     p.      cm.
   Includes bibliographical references and index.
   Summary: A biography of Katherine Dunham, emphasizing her childhood, her love of anthropology and dance, and the creation of her unique dance style.
   ISBN 1–57505–353–5 (lib. bdg.: alk. paper)
   1. Dunham, Katherine—Juvenile literature. 2. Dancers—
United States—Biography—Juvenile literature. 3. Choreographers—
United States—Juvenile literature. [1. Dunham, Katherine.
2. Dancers. 3. Choreographers. 4. Afro-Americans—Biography.] I. Title.
GV1785.D82036 2000
792.8'028'092—dc21                                                         98–50426
[B]

Manufactured in the United States of America
1 2 3 4 5 6 – JR – 05 04 03 02 01 00

# Contents

Katherine Dunham as a young girl

# Hard Times, Good Times

Not many people believed Katherine Dunham when she said she could remember the day she was born— June 22, 1909.  She claimed she could recall lying in a basket in the hospital, crying louder than all the other babies lined up in a row.  And she was certain that on the ride home, while she lay snuggled in her mother's arms, the horse that pulled their carriage had been frightened by a butterfly.

Also tucked away in Katherine's memory were music-filled nights in a lovely gray house in Glen Ellyn, Illinois.  She remembered lying drowsily in her bed, listening to her mother play her harp and her father strum his guitar.

Katherine's mother, Fanny June Dunham, was a pale-skinned woman of French Canadian and American

Fanny June Dunham with Albert Jr.          Albert Dunham Sr.

Indian heritage. When Fanny married Albert Dunham, she
didn't care a bit that he was twenty years younger than
she was or that he was black (although the gossiping
neighbors cared). And when Albert married Fanny, he
didn't care that she had five grown children from a previ-
ous marriage.

Fanny and Albert settled into a two-storied wooden
house in Glen Ellyn shortly after the birth of their son,
Albert Jr., in 1905. Four years later, Katherine came
along. Less than four years after that, in 1913, Fanny
got sick and died. Heartbroken, Albert Sr. sold the house
and got a job as a traveling salesman. Katherine and
her brother were whisked off to live with their father's
sister, Lulu, in a black ghetto on the South Side of
Chicago.

To be snatched up from their happy lives in Glen Ellyn and plunked down in the middle of a run-down, one-room apartment in the slums might have seemed cruel to the two grieving children had it not been for the good heart of Lulu Dunham.  Lulu had a way of making a cold, shabby room seem like a place good enough to call home.  With Lulu there was always plenty of love but never enough money to keep coal in the stove or food in the pantry.  Every morning she hurried Albert out the door and off to school.  Then she and Katherine took the train downtown to Lulu's beauty parlor.

While Lulu cut and curled hair and gave manicures, four-year-old Katherine helped keep the beauty parlor looking nice for Lulu's well-to-do customers.  She liked dusting and polishing, hauling dirty linens to the hall, and then, as she liked to tell it, "putting clean linen in all the wrong places."

When she wasn't helping out, there wasn't much for Katherine to do but sit at a table in the closet, tracing words in her brother's spelling book.  Sometimes she climbed right up on top of the table and took a nap.  Other times she just lay there and thought.  Most of the time, her thoughts were about pleasant, lip-smacking things like the day-old cream puffs Aunt Lulu bought every three days or the tamales sold on the street corner.  But every now and then she had more serious thoughts— thoughts about her beautiful mother who had loved music or about where in the world her daddy was.  Sometimes she thought maybe he'd just up and forgotten about her and Albert.

Such thoughts made Katherine feel sad and alone and anxious to get home to her brother. Albert was only a boy of eight, but in Katherine's eyes, he was a hero. He shooed away the bogeyman from under the bed and, as she recalled in her memoirs, he never tired of answering "her never-ending 'why's' about things and people and events." He had a knack for knowing when she was down in the dumps, and he knew that calling her "Kitty" cheered her up.

Most days it was long after dark by the time Katherine and Lulu left the beauty parlor and started the long trip back home. Katherine sometimes fell asleep on the elevated train until it screeched to a halt at their Thirty-first Street stop. Hurrying along the dark, littered sidewalks, Katherine stayed close to Lulu. Sometimes she peered into the dimly lit apartments they passed, curious about the goings-on inside. Even a quick glimpse told her those run-down, crowded rooms were a world apart from Lulu's spotless downtown beauty shop with its starched white curtains and thick, soft carpets.

The closer they got to home, the quicker Katherine's tired legs moved. The tamale man was just around the corner. Katherine loved his familiar call. "Ta-ma-a-a-a-le! Come git ya tamale! Come git 'em whilst dey hot!" The smell of the hot, spicy meat and cornmeal dough wrapped and steamed in corn husks made Katherine's empty stomach rumble. If she and Lulu didn't hurry, when they got to the brightly painted tamale cart, the tamales would be sold out. When that happened, Katherine didn't know who was more disappointed, she with her empty stomach or a hungry Albert, waiting in their cluttered little room at home.

Sometimes Katherine envied Albert. How lucky he was to go to school with other children, and how smart he was to read all those books. Katherine wasn't sure she would ever be as smart as Albert, but she had a knack for watching and learning from things going on around her. As more and more blacks came to Chicago from the South, Katherine began to notice little things that left big impressions. When she and Aunt Lulu picked up their lunches from the cafeteria below the beauty shop, Katherine noticed the raised eyebrows of the white patrons dining there. When an important-looking man in a blue suit asked Lulu to stop coming to the cafeteria, Katherine noticed Lulu's embarrassment. And when the property owner refused to renew Lulu's lease on the beauty shop, Katherine couldn't help but notice Lulu's tears. Four-year-old Katherine didn't need schoolbooks to teach her that the raised eyebrows, embarrassment, and tears had nothing to do with her aunt's kind heart and everything to do with the color of her skin.

No longer able to rent the downtown beauty shop, Lulu packed up her shampoos and curling irons and manicure kits and took her services to her clients' homes. While Lulu worked, Katherine was passed from one Dunham to another. Katherine later recalled "always catching cold and always [being] underfoot," though she didn't intend to be.

Lulu struggled to take care of her brother's children, but times were hard. To get by, she was forever moving in with an assortment of uncles, aunts, and cousins. The

Dunham clan was a lively bunch who shared a love of the theater.  When Uncle Arthur Dunham, a voice coach, staged a musical drama called *Minnehaha*, Katherine sneaked to the basement to watch rehearsals.  From her hiding place, a wide-eyed Katherine was thrilled to see Aunt Clara and Cousin Irene prancing about in face paint and costumes.  Although *Minnehaha* was not very successful, it left a lasting impression on Katherine.  She later remarked that "memories of that winter...may have inspired in some small way [my] own eventual choice of a theatrical career."

When Lulu packed up the children and moved in with a second cousin, Katherine got another taste of show business.  While Lulu worked and Albert was at school,

Albert Jr. *(left)* and Katherine *(right)* were close.  Katherine looked up to her wise, older brother.

Katherine skipped along beside her cousin to the vaude-ville stage shows at Chicago theaters like the Monogram and the Grand. With the money Lulu had scraped to-gether for food and coal, the cousin instead bought tickets to see her favorite performers. Perched on her cousin's lap, Katherine was awed by the singing of Bessie Smith and Ethel Waters. She grinned till her cheeks ached watching the dance and comedy acts of Cole and Johnson or Buck and Bubbles.

Back home after the show, the cousin lit the coal stove. Katherine fanned the heat around the cold apartment before Lulu returned and learned that her hard-earned pen-nies had bought tickets not food or coal. Stale bread steamed over a kettle kept Katherine satisfied until Lulu brought home cold meats and sweet rolls.

For the poor folks on Chicago's South Side, winters were long and cruel. Katherine recalled that the winter of 1914 was unusually cold. On the worst mornings, she and Albert would sit by the lighted gas oven. They would huddle under a blanket and peer through the ice-coated window at the streets below. For Katherine, having Albert home from school was worth a little shivering. She loved to talk, and Albert was more fun to talk to than their cousin. Although Albert didn't say much, "what he said was always wise." Katherine wanted nothing more than to please him.

With a wise brother to look up to and a good-hearted aunt to love her, Katherine found life pretty good. But "on the coldest day of all," Fanny June Weir "swept into the basement flat" and changed everything.

Joliet, Illinois—Katherine's childhood hometown—in 1914

# A Not-So-Happy Home

Fanny June Weir, the daughter of Fanny Dunham by her first marriage, inspected the shabby apartment with a disapproving scowl. She took one look at the dirty kitchen, the empty pantry, and the two bewildered children shivering by the oven and decided that Katherine and Albert would be better off living with her. Ignoring Albert's protests, she hurried the children outside and into a waiting taxi. "Before we knew it," Katherine wrote in her memoirs, "we had passed out of neighborhoods familiar to us." Once again Katherine found herself plucked from a home she loved. This time, however, she wasn't welcomed with loving arms. Fanny June Weir "was quick-tempered and a firm believer in adult authority."

In the Weir home, Katherine felt "shy and embar-rassed." Fanny June's light-skinned children teased her about her kinky hair and darker skin. When she gobbled up the plentiful food at dinnertime, they glared with dis-approval and called her greedy. Not a day went by that she wasn't reminded that she was "all black" and they were "near white." It didn't take long for Katherine to re-alize that she'd rather be cold and hungry with Lulu than warm and well fed with the uppity Weirs.

When Albert Sr. learned of Fanny June's doings, he joined forces with Lulu to get the children back. But Fanny June put up a fight. The battle ended up in a court-room, the Weirs on one side, the Dunhams on the other. Scared and confused, Katherine and Albert Jr. were in the middle. A judge listened to tales of empty coal stoves, stale bread, and little Katherine's afternoons in the Mono-gram Theater. Then he ordered that the children stay with Fanny June until their father could provide a better home for them.

Katherine spent the next unhappy year trying to get along with her relatives. Then one wintry day in early 1915, a letter came with some surprising news. Albert Sr. had a new dry-cleaning business—and a new wife! He was coming to take the children to their new home in Joliet, Illinois, forty miles outside Chicago.

Katherine was delighted to say good-bye to the ill-tempered Fanny June and her unpleasant clan. But a new mother? Katherine wasn't sure what to think about that. How could a new mother ever be as wonderful as the beautiful, harp-playing mother in her memories?

Katherine's worries were soon over.  The new Mrs. Dunham was a former schoolteacher named Annette Poindexter.  Katherine liked her just fine.  She wasn't beautiful and she didn't play the harp, but she was "fiercely loyal to the children and as full of mother love as a human being can be."

Sadly, Albert Sr. wasn't the same happy man that Katherine remembered.  She longed to snuggle into his lap and listen to stories of Br'er Rabbit and the Tar Baby like she used to, but her father had no time for that anymore.  He was determined to see his new business grow and prosper, and he expected his family to help him.  His stern face, never-ending list of chores, and frequent use of a leather strap on bare legs told Katherine that things had changed.

Sometimes at night, lying on her cot in the back room of the West Side Cleaners and Dyers, Katherine listened hopefully for the pleasant sound of her father's guitar. But most nights, all she heard was the whirring of Annette's sewing machine as she did the alterations for the shop. Before long, the muffled sound of her parents' arguing drifted through the walls, too.

Katherine spent her days sewing name tags into customers' clothing and keeping one eye on the clock, counting the minutes until her brother returned from school.  But most days, Albert Jr. barely had time to say "Hey, Kitty." Then he was off to make deliveries for the store, leaving Katherine alone again to daydream.  In her dreams, her brother "could spend more time with her, as he had long ago, and her mother wouldn't look so worried

Annette Poindexter married Katherine's father in 1915.

all the time, and her father would be friendly again and tell stories about the Tar Baby on Sunday nights."

That fall Katherine was finally old enough to escape the boring, smelly dry-cleaning shop and head off to school. She liked school. But she knew right away that she would never bring home the excellent report cards that Albert did. Katherine was good at other things, though, like sports and music and thinking up ways to make friends and attract attention. When she was ten and yearning for a little "belongingness" at school, Katherine formed the Eagle Eye Society. She invited two or three lucky girls to join this secret club. Katherine was president. She made each club member a red satin headband with beads sewn on it in the shape of an eye. The girls wore the headbands so that the eye stared boldly from the center of their foreheads. The Eagle Eye Society was the envy of the fifth grade until teachers complained. The headbands were forbidden, and Katherine's popularity dwindled as quickly as it had grown.

At home the mood grew tenser as the family business grew. The Dunhams had expanded the business to include rug and carpet cleaning and had moved into the apartment over the shop. When Katherine's family wasn't working, they were arguing. According to Albert Sr., his wife worked too little and complained too much. His son spent too much time doing schoolwork and not enough time learning the family business.

Katherine did her best to stay out of the way and avoid her father's angry eyes. She had long since given up listening for music at night. The sound of fussing and fighting and hitting and crying kept her stomach so balled up she could hardly sleep.

By 1922, the year she entered high school, Katherine was tall and athletic. It was only natural, then, that she played basketball and ran on the track team. But more than anything, Katherine wanted to join the school's Terpsichorean Club, a performing group that put on dances and musicals. Katherine loved to watch dancing and thought that she would be good at it if she had a chance. "I was always thinking in terms of rhythm and motion," she later recalled.

Katherine Dunham in her teen years

Katherine hoped to get a chance to audition for the club. Before she auditioned, she was allowed to perform some minor roles as "an eager wood nymph, a willing tree, and an obliging scarf bearer" in a recital. In the same recital, she watched another dancer leap and twirl in a lively performance of a Russian dance called the *hopak.* Katherine made up her mind right then and there. She would learn that Russian dance. It took some doing, but Katherine persuaded her parents to let her take dance classes after school. She learned to leap and skip and wave her arms to the beat of a drum. But disappointingly, she wasn't taught the hopak. Still, she auditioned and was accepted into the Terpsichorean Club the following term.

About the same time, Katherine attended a meeting at her church—Brown's Chapel, an African Methodist Episcopal church. At the meeting, church members discussed ways to raise money for a new parish house. Some suggested a fish fry, others a barbecue or a fashion show. Before her practical side could tell her to sit still and keep quiet, Katherine was waving her hand in the air. "I would like to organize a cabaret party," she announced.

Half of the church members sat in "stunned silence." They wondered how a fourteen-year-old girl could even know what a cabaret was, much less plan one. But Katherine had always been a good listener. When the highfalutin Weir clan had told stories about being in fancy cabarets (little cafés where people ate, drank, and watched a variety of entertainers), Katherine had soaked up every detail. She knew all about them, she assured the church members. And she could practically guarantee

Cabarets were popular in the 1920s.  Lively musicians, such as McKie Fitzhugh *(far left)* and Willie Dixon *(second from left)*, entertained audiences across the United States.

that theirs would be a success, because she herself would produce it, direct it, and, of course, star in it.

Enthusiasm for Katherine's cabaret spread as church members sewed costumes, made refreshments, and rehearsed their favorite songs and dances.  Tickets sold so quickly that even the most disapproving church elders were impressed.  The sold-out Blue Moon Café "was considered an outstanding success."  The highlight of the evening was Katherine Dunham, leaping and twirling in her own version of the Russian hopak. She performed so brilliantly that the audience demanded an encore, which Katherine was delighted to give.

Shortly after the success of the cabaret, Katherine got some devastating news. Her brother was leaving home. He had won a scholarship to study at the University of Chicago. "The bottom fell out of everything" for Katherine. How could she face each day without her beloved brother? Despite Albert's promises to help her, too, leave home someday, "a spark had gone from her. . . . At fourteen, she felt old and tired."

Katherine as a young adult

# The Great Wide World

On a cold March day in 1925, Katherine and her step-mother, Annette, decided they had had enough of Albert Sr. They packed their bags and marched downstairs, through the dry cleaners, and right out the front door. Father "worked steadily at his pressing machine and did not look up at [our] departure," Katherine recalled. "There were no farewells."

The two Dunham women rented a little house on Elmwood Avenue and started their new life. They quickly realized that while they were free of Albert's temper, they were also without his money. Annette's few sewing jobs couldn't support them, so fifteen-year-old Katherine reluctantly went back to work in the dry-cleaning shop after school.

Katherine had little time left for sports, dance lessons, the Terpsichorean Club, or William Booker, the football player who had taken a shine to her. William liked to walk with Katherine from school to the bridge that led to Bluff Street, but her father made sure he went no farther.

Katherine finished high school in 1926 and started classes at a nearby junior college.  Still, she was allowed only one Saturday afternoon a month for school social activities.  Dating was out of the question.  Even after Katherine turned eighteen, her father remained firm.  Under no circumstances would his daughter go out with boys.

Katherine hated her father's harsh rules.  It seemed as though nearly every girl she knew went to football games and parties with a boyfriend.  Not Katherine.  She spent her Saturdays reading at the library.  But William Booker was persistent.  He continued to ask Katherine out, and Katherine continued to refuse.  Finally, she confessed to the frustrated young man that her father would not allow her to date.  When William heard that, he went straight over to West Side Cleaners and Dyers and asked Albert Dunham for permission to take Katherine to a basketball game.  Albert's answer was a loud and clear "No!" Then he "jammed on his battered felt hat and tore through the streets in the delivery wagon to Elmwood Avenue" to confront Katherine.

The sight of her father's face "distorted with fury," the sound of his "bitter words," and the sting of his hand on her face were the last straw for Katherine.  "This is the last time," she told herself.  "The last time he will ever touch me."

The next day, Katherine was on a train to Chicago, feeling freer and happier with each mile that separated her from Joliet.

With her brother's help, Katherine found an apartment, a job at Hamilton Park Branch Library, and the confidence to enroll in classes at the University of Chicago. But she was still more interested in dance than anything else. So she made sure her schedule left time for ballet and tap-dancing classes.

"The great wide world opened before her," and Katherine charged into it full steam ahead. On the first day of her new job, she marched proudly into the library and introduced herself to the staff. She had expected a warm welcome. Instead, she was greeted with frozen smiles, slight nods, and strange looks. The test that Katherine had taken when she applied for the job had told her employer that she was bright and qualified—not that she was black. But Katherine was too excited about her new life to give much thought to the reason for this

Albert Dunham Jr. in his high school graduation portrait

unexpectedly cold reception. Not even eating lunch alone or being isolated in a back room to work could dampen Katherine's spirits.

Free at last from her father's watchful eye, Katherine hardly knew what to do first. There were plays to see, concerts to attend, and literary discussion groups in which to take part. Before long, Katherine had a circle of varied and colorful friends. She was especially fond of a bright young student named Frances Taylor. The two shared interests in dance and theater, and eventually became roommates.

Katherine and Frances enrolled in ballet classes with a Russian woman named Ludmila Speranzeva. In Ludmila's classes, Katherine was introduced to an unusual form of ballet that emphasized acting and storytelling through dance. Katherine was intrigued by this dance form and inspired by Ludmila's teaching. Sometimes she daydreamed about becoming a dance teacher herself.

Despite her busy schedule, Katherine managed to squeeze in some time for her brother. Albert dropped by often, and soon Katherine realized he wasn't just coming by to visit her. He and Frances struck up a friendship that quickly turned to romance. Albert won a grant (a gift of money) to pursue his graduate studies at Harvard University, in Massachusetts. He surprised Katherine by announcing that Frances would be going with him—as his wife! On September 13, 1929, Katherine posed for wedding photos beside her beaming brother and her best friend.

Alone for the first time, Katherine continued her classes at the university and worked hard at her library job. But the best part of her day was dance class. She be-

The dancer and choreographer Ruth Page helped Katherine get her start as a teacher.

gan to think that maybe she could combine her love of dancing with her need to earn money by opening a dance school. But how? She had no money, no studio, and no students. Lucky for Katherine, she had two enthusiastic friends who shared her love of dance. Choreographer Ruth Page and ballet dancer Mark Turbyfill helped Katherine carry out her plan. Ruth gave Katherine enough money to rent a small studio, and Mark offered to teach classes without pay.

When Katherine opened the door to her new school early in 1930, at the age of twenty, she had a clear vision of what she hoped to accomplish. Since her childhood days in the darkened Monogram Theater, Katherine had been inspired by the unique style of black entertainers. Why not teach dance that emphasized that style?

Chicago in the early 1930s was a bustling city with a growing black population. The sudden popularity of black music, dancing, and writing among whites had created a growth in the arts, called the Harlem Renaissance. (The word *renaissance* means a period of time when great developments are made in the arts and sciences.) Katherine thought that maybe the time was right for a school that emphasized black dance styles. She also hoped to form a black concert dance troupe. At that time, most dance groups performed only in musical comedies or as part of song-and-dance variety shows rather than concert dances

Katherine Dunham works with her students.

(stage performances devoted completely to dancing). The few concert dance groups Katherine knew about were white groups performing classical ballet. There were no black concert dance companies from which to get ideas. So Katherine would have to rely mostly on classical ballet. She decided to call her small group of dance students Ballet Nègre (French for Negro Ballet).

Katherine spent the next year working with Ballet Nègre. She was a natural at teaching and choreography (planning the movements that make up a dance). When her dance troupe was invited to perform at Chicago's Beaux Arts Ball, Katherine was thrilled. She choreographed a special dance for the event called "Negro Rhapsody." The performance was well liked, but it didn't receive the raves she had hoped for. Katherine's students were disappointed, too. Some began to drop out of the group. When Ruth and Mark were no longer able to help, Katherine had no choice but to close her school.

About this time, Katherine became friends with a young dancer named Jordis McCoo. She liked him so much, she up and married him! By the time Katherine sat down to have a long think about what she had done, she was already a married woman. But Katherine wasn't about to let marriage slow her down. She went looking for a way to teach dance again. If determination were enough to run a successful dance school, Katherine would have had no trouble. But it took money and students, and she was having a hard time finding either one.

Sometimes Katherine got discouraged. Had she been wrong to think she could teach dance? Was her idea of a black concert dance group crazy?  Maybe people just weren't ready for her new ideas.

Just when she was beginning to doubt her dreams, something happened to set her back on track.  She attended a lecture by Dr. Robert Redfield, a professor at the university.  Dr. Redfield taught anthropology—the study of human origins, beliefs, and customs.  He specialized in American Indian and African culture.

In his studies, Dr. Redfield had found that much of black culture in modern America had begun in Africa and had been handed down from generation to generation.  Even during slavery, blacks had managed to pass on their African customs, religious beliefs, music, and dance.  Katherine was especially excited to learn that some of the most popular American dance steps at that time, like the lindy hop and the cakewalk, could be traced back more than seventy years to tribal dances in Africa.  Here was something worth listening to!  African dances had been brought to America by slaves and handed down through generations!

Katherine left Dr. Redfield's lecture that day with a plan.  She would major in anthropology and learn all she could about the roots of African American dance.  She would compare the modern dances of Africa and America and connect young black dancers with their African heritage.

When Katherine told her friend Ludmila about her ideas, the dance teacher was excited, too.  She encouraged Katherine to teach modern dance rather than ballet.  Modern dance was less formal and more expressive.  Ludmila offered to let Katherine use her studio to teach.  Katherine announced her new Negro Dance Group, then waited hopefully for black dancers to enroll. The group didn't live up to her hopes. Parents complained that Katherine worked her students too hard, demanding long hours of training and rehearsal. And most of the black parents who visited her school wanted their children to learn classical ballet, not African dances.

But Katherine wasn't about to let some misunderstanding parents squelch her interest in African dance. Every chance she got, she talked about tracing the roots of black dance. Her friends thought her ideas were exciting, and they encouraged her.

When Ruth Page composed a ballet based on a Caribbean folktale, she asked Katherine to dance the lead role. Katherine didn't hesitate to accept the part. When *La Guiablesse* (The Devil Woman) opened at the Chicago Opera House, Katherine danced a stunning performance. Her parents watched proudly from the audience. Since Katherine had left home, her father had found he missed his family and had softened his hard ways enough to convince Annette to come back to him. Attending Katherine's performance was perhaps Albert's way of trying to patch things up with his daughter.

After Katherine's successful performance in Ruth's ballet, the dance community began to listen more closely to Katherine's ideas about black dance. In 1933 she was hired to train 150 black dancers to perform at the Chicago World's Fair. Katherine could hardly believe her good luck! Scarcely a year before, her classes in black dance hadn't been able to interest enough students to keep her

Millions of people attended the 1933 Chicago World's Fair, an exhibit of technology, industry, and culture.

school open.  Now she was being given students *because* of her unique style!

The more Katherine worked with black dancers, the more determined she was to research the roots of African dance.  She had been taking anthropology classes since attending Dr. Redfield's lecture, but something was still missing.  Anthropologists could teach her that African dance was used to communicate and to carry on traditions.  But could they show her the dances?  Could they describe the rhythms?  Could they tell the stories the dances told?  Katherine knew that to really learn about traditional African dance, she would need to learn the dances herself—from the people who danced them.

More determined than ever, Katherine applied for financial help from the Julius Rosenwald Foundation, an organization that often gave grants to artists to pursue their studies.  Katherine put a lot of thought and worry into how to present her ideas to the foundation.  When the day came, Katherine dressed in a plain jacket and skirt and appeared before the solemn-faced judges. Then, stripping down to the leotard and tights she wore beneath her street clothes, Katherine twisted, leaped, and rolled about the room in her own version of an African war dance.

"I want to go where they dance like that," she told the surprised judges when she had finished. "I want to find out why, how it started, and what influence it had on the people."

Katherine's dramatic presentation worked the way she'd hoped it would. On February 15, 1935, she learned she had been awarded a grant to cover her travel expenses. Katherine Dunham's career was about to begin.

Katherine *(far right)* with some Haitian friends around 1935

# Caribbean Adventure

About the same time that Katherine got the good news about the grant, she got bad news about her brother. Albert had suffered a mental breakdown. Katherine felt sad and helpless. If only she could cheer him up the way his "Hey, Kitty" had cheered her as a child. Realizing she couldn't help him, however, Katherine concentrated on her plan to study black dance.

The Rosenwald Foundation had suggested that Katherine begin her studies in the West Indies. This group of islands in the Caribbean Sea (an arm of the Atlantic Ocean) had large populations of Africans. Katherine thought that was a fine idea. The grant would provide her with enough money to spend nearly a year studying on four islands. But before she could begin her travels, she was required to spend several months taking courses from Dr. Melville Herskovits, head of the Department of

Dr. Herskovits

Anthropology and African Studies at Northwestern University, near Chicago.  Katherine didn't care much for that idea.  She had spent enough time sitting in classrooms.  Unless Dr. Herskovits could dance, Katherine felt sure that studying with him would be just a waste of time.

She was wrong.  Dr. Herskovits had made many field trips to Africa and the Caribbean.  He knew from experience what Katherine was in for.  The tropical jungles of the West Indies were a long way from the city streets of Chicago.  Katherine would experience a new climate, new foods, new customs, and new diseases.  She would be staying in places that had no hospitals, no indoor toilets, and no electricity.  Katherine had a lot to learn about taking care of herself in the strange new places she would be calling home.

Dr. Herskovits was a knowledgeable and enthusiastic teacher. He helped Katherine understand that to study African dance meant learning about many other aspects of African culture as well, from dress to customs to religion. These things can all play a part in the appearance or meaning of a dance. Dr. Herskovits also reminded Katherine that when she returned to school, she would have to report on what she had learned and observed. It was important, then, that she know how to take notes, write reports, make tape recordings, and use both still cameras and movie cameras.

When Katherine realized how much preparation was needed for her trip, she was grateful for the time she spent with Dr. Herskovits. But before the eager student rushed off on her new adventure, the professor had one more important piece of advice. Slow down, he told her. To gain the respect and trust of the West Indians would take time. For twenty-five-year-old Katherine Dunham, anxious to begin fulfilling a dream, the words "slow down" were hard words to hear.

By the summer of 1935, Katherine's head was packed with countless things to remember. Her bags were packed with medicines, notebooks, cameras, tape recorders, and letters of introduction from Dr. Herskovits. Katherine said good-bye to Jordis and her other friends in Chicago and took a plane, a boat, a train, and a car to the town of Whitehall, in Jamaica. From there she rode a donkey up a winding trail to the tiny mountain village of

Accompong. Along the way, the air was thick with the sweet smell of mango, and the long leaves of banana trees shaded the path.

Katherine watched in fascination as villagers gracefully climbed the rugged mountain trail with her luggage balanced on their heads. At the top of the mountain, Katherine slid off her donkey and greeted the crowd of curious people gathered around her. Called the Maroons, the people of Accompong were descended from Africans captured and taken to Jamaica to work in the sugarcane fields.

That night Katherine lay on a straw mat on the floor of a grass hut, listening to the sounds of the jungle around her. The Maroons had a reputation for being fierce and distant, so outsiders knew little about their culture. Katherine wondered if the people would ever trust her enough to show her some of their traditional dances. Suddenly, her thoughts were interrupted by the sound of Benny Goodman's jazz music blaring from somewhere outside her hut. Some of the villagers had gotten into her luggage and were playing her records! Katherine must have realized then that the Maroons were as curious about her as she was about them. Maybe they weren't so fierce after all.

Katherine spent her first few days in Accompong getting used to the spicy tropical food, decorating her hut with bowls of gardenias, and trying to make friends with the villagers. The Maroons liked this friendly American woman. She laughed at their stories and played her records for them. At night, her hut glowed with the light of a kerosene lamp while she scribbled furiously in her notebook.

Soon Katherine's brief stay in Jamaica was over. During her visit, she had been able to watch only two traditional African dances, but they were dances she would never forget. In the glow of kerosene torches, an elderly man and woman performed a war dance to the beat of a *goombay,* a square, wooden drum. The dance told the story of a witch doctor trying to gain the knowledge of black magic from a dead woman. The terrified witch doctor crouched in fear as the dead woman circled him, then hovered over him until the dance ended with one final beat of the goombay.

The villagers also performed a war dance called the Koromantee. Moving to the drumbeat, the men swung clubs at their invisible enemies. The women urged the men into their imaginary battle by shaking rattles in their faces. The war dance ended with the women taking kerchiefs off their heads and waving them in victory.

When Katherine packed to leave Jamaica, she added new treasures to her already stuffed bags. She had bought herself a reed basket, a wooden bowl, and a hammock. But her most prized mementos from Jamaica were the African musical instruments her new friends had given her, including a bamboo flute, a gourd rattle, and her very own goombay.

From Accompong, Katherine went to Martinique, another West Indian island. There she was introduced to another war dance called Ag'Ya. Katherine was intrigued by the dance and tried hard to memorize all the movements. Later in her career, her version of Ag'Ya would become one of her most popular performances.

Katherine's next stop was Trinidad, where she heard about a secret religious ceremony once performed in Africa and brought to Trinidad by slaves. During the ceremony, the locals danced imitations of animals in honor of Shango, the god of thunder and lightning. Katherine was determined to film this ancient ceremony. With the help of a friend, she met a Shango priest who agreed to let her watch the ritual from the window of a nearby hut. When the ceremony got under way, Katherine was amazed to see the priest take up a squawking rooster in one hand and a shiny knife in the other. Katherine had heard about animal sacrifices (animals killed as gifts to a god), but she had never seen one. With trembling hands, she aimed her camera out the window. When the priest heard the whirring of the camera, he threw the rooster and the knife in the air, burst into the hut, and angrily yanked the camera from Katherine. For the rest of her trip, she left her camera in her suitcase.

After her brief glimpse of the Shango ceremony, Katherine was even more curious about the ancient religious rites of the African peoples. These rituals interested her as an anthropologist as well as a dancer. But she also realized that they were a valuable part of her own heritage.

Early in 1936, Katherine made the final stop of her field trip—Haiti, a beautiful country on the Caribbean island of Hispaniola. From the moment she stepped onto the sparkling shores and gazed at the palm groves and poinsettia bushes around her, Katherine knew she had found her heart's home. She didn't know why, she later remarked, she just fell in love with Haiti from the start.

To her delight, Katherine found that Haiti was just what she had been looking for—a place where Africans still lived much the same as their ancestors had hundreds of years before them. The blacks in Haiti were descended from West Africans brought to the island as slaves by the French and Spanish. These blacks still practiced many of the customs handed down to them, including the religion of *vodun,* which is commonly known in the United States as voodoo. This religion combines Roman Catholicism with traditional African religions.

Gaining the trust and friendship of the Haitians came easily for Katherine. Her relaxed and easy manner as she ate from the common cooking pot with them made even the most suspicious villager warm to her. But Katherine remembered Dr. Herskovits's warning to go slow. Rather than bombard her new friends with the endless questions

Drummers perform in a voodoo ritual *(left)*. In Haiti voodoo dancers dance in a hypnotic state *(right)*.

building in her head, Katherine traded face powder and cologne, chatted with them about local gossip, and danced with them by firelight. The Haitians couldn't help but like this energetic American anthropologist.

Katherine grew especially close to three women— Téoline, Dégrasse, and Cécile. Téoline and Dégrasse were *mambos,* or voodoo priestesses. Katherine was eager to learn about the religion from them and to see some of their ceremonial dances. But "go slow" echoed in her head. She would wait until the time was right.

Often Katherine would look out her hotel window and see one of her new friends waiting in the street below. Katherine would wave cheerfully and run down to greet them. Her friends didn't dare come inside the hotel because of the darkness of their skin. Katherine was welcome because her skin was lighter and more acceptable to the light-skinned, upper-class Haitians who stayed at the hotel. When Katherine chatted with Téoline on a park bench or strolled through the city with Dégrasse, she ignored the glares of disapproval from passersby. But inside she burned with anger. Katherine had known the hurt of racism as far back as her days with Fanny June Weir's children. She would never choose her friends based on the color of their skin.

As the weeks went by, Katherine learned more about the different cultures of Haiti. She visited the country villages often, especially the village of Cul-de-Sac, in the hills overlooking Port-au-Prince (Haiti's capital). Soon she was a welcome and trusted visitor there. The people she met in Haiti knew she was interested in their religious

Katherine's dance company performs in 1936.

ceremonies and dances, and sometimes they invited her to watch.

Once Katherine was invited to stay in the hut of her friend Antoine during a ceremony that was to last several days. "I was about to settle comfortably on the floor mat indicated by my host," she later recalled, "when I noticed an odor which never fails to set the hairs on the back of my neck on end." The odor was that of a snake—an eight-foot python, to be exact—curled around the rafters over her head. (Many Haitians kept snakes in their homes to eat rats and mice.) Katherine froze in fear. She wanted to be a polite guest, but that beady-eyed snake with the darting tongue was too much. "Because of it," she wrote, "my night was sleepless and because of it I left early the next morning in a downpour of rain."

Several weeks later, Katherine finally got what she had been hoping for—an invitation to take part in a voodoo initiation ceremony. An important element of voodoo is the worship of spirits, or saints, called *loas.* Katherine knew that African dancing, drumming, and singing were part of the voodoo ceremony. She wanted to learn more about voodoo. "To know the dances of Haiti," Katherine later wrote, "the life surrounding the dances must be known, and the focus of this life is the vodun."

According to voodoo belief, once Katherine was possessed by her loa, she would lose her own identity and would behave like the loa until the spell was broken at the end of the ceremony. Katherine learned from her friend Dégrasse that her loa was to be Damballa, the snake god! She didn't know whether to be scared or excited.

Before the ceremony, Katherine had to collect offerings for her loa—beads, barley water, strawberry soda, sugar cookies, eggs, herbs, roots, and two live roosters. Then she dressed in special white clothing and matted her hair with a paste of eggs and cornmeal. She lay on the dirt floor of a hut for three days, moving only when she heard hands clap or a bell ring. (Only then was she allowed to turn over or get up to use the toilet.) Her empty stomach rumbled and her muscles ached.

Outside the hut, drums beat day and night. Finally, into the hut came a Haitian drummer, slithering along the floor on his belly. As his tongue darted in and out of his mouth, he approached a saucer containing flour and a raw egg, the voodoo offering for Damballa. The loa ate the egg and then slithered out of the hut. Katherine was fascinated, but she didn't feel possessed by her loa.

The ritual ended with a feast and dancing. Katherine studied the movements of the voodoo worshipers as they jerked their shoulders forward and back to the beat of the drums. Then she returned to her hotel, hungry and exhausted. With her hair still matted with cornmeal paste, Katherine sat down to make notes on every detail of the dances she had seen.

Late in the spring of 1936, Katherine prepared to return to Chicago to continue her studies at the university. She said a sad good-bye to her friends in the hills. Walking back to Port-au-Prince to collect her belongings, Katherine stopped at a spring to drink water and chat with a group of women gathered there. The clear, cool water ran down the mountain from the grounds of a crumbling, deserted mansion believed by many Haitians to be haunted. Called Habitation Leclerc, the home looked beautiful to Katherine. The rest of the way back to the hotel, Katherine couldn't get the old mansion out of her head. Maybe someday, she thought, she would return to Haiti and buy Habitation Leclerc.

As her boat pulled away from the shores of Haiti, Katherine gazed out at the beautiful countryside. She was returning to the United States with musical instruments, tape recordings of drumming, photos of dancing, and pages of notes. Yet somehow, she felt she was leaving part of herself behind.

Katherine Dunham and Rex Ingram perform in the musical *Cabin in the Sky.*

# From Haiti to Harlem

When Katherine presented the results of her Caribbean studies to the Julius Rosenwald Foundation in June of 1936, she did it in true Dunham style. No boring speeches for her! Instead, she showed pictures, played tape recordings, and danced a dramatic imitation of her old friend Damballa the snake while Dr. Herskovits played the drums. Katherine's entertaining presentation showed that she had found a definite connection between dance and other forms of African culture. The intrigued members of the foundation were satisfied that she had used their grant money well.

That August Katherine received her degree in social anthropology from the University of Chicago. Shortly after that, she learned that she had been awarded a grant from the Rockefeller Foundation to continue her studies with

Dr. Herskovits. Part of Katherine was pleased. But another part of her was confused and uncertain. She was both an anthropologist and a dancer. She could choose to build a career talking about African dance in a classroom, or she could dance it on a stage.

Dr. Herskovits expected her to follow in his footsteps and teach. She knew that teaching would provide her with the regular income that dancing probably would not. But the dancer in Katherine was putting up a fight. She wanted to show the world the unique style and cultural value of black dance. Katherine wished she could talk to her brother about her dilemma, but he was still hospitalized and dealing with his own troubles.

About the same time, Katherine faced another problem. She and Jordis had spent little time together during their five years of marriage and had grown apart. They decided to separate.

While Katherine tried to make up her mind about continuing her studies with Dr. Herskovits, she gratefully returned to the dance studio, full of new ideas and energy. With Ludmila's help, the Negro Dance Group had stayed together while Katherine was gone. She was eager to teach the students some of the dances she had learned in the West Indies.

In March 1937, the dance troupe was invited to New York to perform in a program called Negro Dance Evening. Katherine knew this was her chance to showcase some of her new work. Katherine Dunham and the dance company loaded two old cars with their costumes and musical instruments and set off on a snowy, fifteen-hour drive to New York. They performed a modern ballet, then moved on to several Haitian dances. The audience loved them.

The success of her first black dances in New York gave Katherine just the yank she needed in the tug-of-war between dancing and teaching. Dance had won. Her stomach knotted up with guilt, Katherine called Dr. Herskovits. She was a dancer, she told him. She appreciated his help with her studies. She was grateful for his support. But she didn't belong in a classroom. The silence on the other end of the phone told her what she already knew. Dr. Herskovits was disappointed. Katherine felt bad about hurting her teacher and friend, but she was relieved that she had finally made her decision.

Katherine put all her energy into carrying out her dream of promoting black dance. She took a job as dance director of Chicago's Federal Theater Project, a government-sponsored arts program. Katherine's new dance group performed its first recital on January 27, 1938. The hit of the evening was "L'Ag'Ya," Katherine's version of the African fighting dance she had seen in Martinique. More than just a dance, "L'Ag'Ya" told the story of two men in love with the same woman. Katherine added plenty of excitement to her choreography. The woman danced wildly under the spell of a voodoo love charm, and the men danced a duel. The primitive dancing, the drumming, and the tropical African costumes were unlike anything audiences had ever seen.

Newspaper critics liked everything about "L'Ag'Ya." Reviewers also mentioned the unique work of John Pratt,

"L'Ag'Ya" was a huge success. Audiences and reviewers loved the excitement that Katherine brought to her version of a Martinican fighting dance.

the man who had designed the costumes. John was a tall, white Canadian who had recently joined Katherine's group as its set and costume designer. As an artist, John admired and respected Katherine's work. Katherine appreciated John's talent. They made a good team. Katherine's success with "L'Ag'Ya" reassured her that her decision to dance instead of teach had been the right one. She hired a manager and took her group, the Dunham Dance Company, on the road.

Katherine spent the year of 1938 packing and unpacking, rehearsing all day, performing at night, and catching

John Pratt and Katherine Dunham were married in 1939.

a little sleep on the way to the next town. Somewhere in her busy schedule, she found time to fall in love with John Pratt. By the end of the year, Katherine had divorced Jordis. On July 10, 1939, she married John. Katherine was aware that her marriage to a white man would set more than a few heads wagging in disapproval. But, as always, Katherine turned a cold shoulder to racial prejudice and did as she pleased.

In the fall of 1939, thirty-year-old Katherine took a job in New York as dance director for a musical called *Pins and Needles.* Every payday she tucked away some money. Finally, she had enough to rent a theater where her dance troupe could perform.

Katherine stars in *Tropics and Le Jazz Hot: From Haiti to Harlem.*

On February 18, 1940, the Dunham Dance Company performed Katherine's choreographed dances in the Windsor Theater on West Forty-eighth Street. The show was called *Tropics and Le Jazz Hot: From Haiti to Harlem.* It included a Cuban rumba, a Mexican rumba, some South American dances, and a folk ballet called *Br'er Rabbit and de Tah Baby.* Katherine was definitely the star of the show. She shimmied her shoulders and swiveled her hips in a dance called "Florida Swamp Shimmy." In another, called "Shore Excursion," she carried a birdcage and danced with a huge cigar in her mouth. The next day, one New York newspaper reported that "Katherine Dunham flared into unsuspecting New York last night like a comet." John's costumes, "as brightly colored as tropical birds," also attracted attention.

Katherine had hoped that, besides enjoying her performance, critics would recognize black dance as a serious art. They did. The *New York Herald Tribune* wrote, "Katherine Dunham has proved herself the first pioneer of the Negro dance." The *New York Times* reported that the development of "Negro dance art . . . look[s] decidedly bright." Katherine's dance company performed *Tropics and Le Jazz Hot* every Sunday for thirteen weeks.

Then came another opportunity for Katherine and her dancers. In August 1940, they performed in an all-black musical called *Cabin in the Sky.* In the role of Georgia Brown, Katherine got to act, sing, and dance. The star of the show was Ethel Waters, one of the singers Katherine had watched from her cousin's lap years ago in Chicago at the Monogram Theater!

After five months on Broadway in New York, *Cabin in the Sky* went on tour. When the show opened in Chicago, Dr. Melville Herskovits sat in the audience and watched his former student perform. The next day, Katherine nervously opened a letter from him. She still felt bad that she had disappointed him by not continuing her studies. To her relief, Dr. Herskovits wrote, "I think you were very wise to concentrate on your dancing and while it may have been nice to have you here, I feel you are taking by far the better course."

Roger Ohardieno and Katherine Dunham in *Barrelhouse*, 1943

# Dancer, Director, Choreographer, & Mother Hen

When *Cabin in the Sky* closed in San Francisco in 1941, Katherine took her dancers south to Hollywood, California. Gazing out her window at the sparkling blue Pacific Ocean and feeling the warm breeze on her face, Katherine couldn't help but think about Haiti. Some day, she promised herself for the umpteenth time, she would go back. But until then, she and John and the dance company had to stay put.

Hollywood moviemakers wanted their movies to be authentic—or so it seemed. The need for black dancers in the movies and Katherine's growing reputation as a choreographer meant jobs and money for the Dunham Dance

Katherine was called in as an expert to oversee the dances in *Pardon My Sarong.*

Company.  When directors needed a Caribbean or African dance, they knew that Katherine Dunham was the expert to call.  In fact, the director of *Pardon My Sarong* called Katherine in as an expert on the dances of Tahiti, an island in the South Pacific Ocean.  Katherine realized the director must have mistaken Haiti for Tahiti, but she needed the job and kept her mouth shut.

Wearing costumes John had designed, Katherine and her group danced in several other movies as well, including *Stormy Weather, Star Spangled Rhythm,* and the movie version of *Cabin in the Sky.*  Katherine was proud to be working with such up-and-coming black performers as Lena Horne and Bojangles Robinson.  She hoped the time had finally come for black entertainers to gain the attention and respect they deserved.  But she had barely unpacked her suitcases when she realized the truth. Movie producers wanted black entertainers, but they didn't want them too black.  The "ideal black dancer" in Hollywood, Katherine later recalled, "was light-skinned."

Katherine was used to racism, but it still irked her. She was proud that there was no hint of prejudice in her dance company. "We had Cubans, West Indians, Latin Americans, and their complexion didn't matter," she said. "What mattered was their talent."

A year after their arrival in California, Katherine and her dance company hit the road again, this time touring in a show they called *Tropical Revue*. Racial prejudice followed them like a shadow. Hotels turned the road-weary dancers away, and restaurants refused to serve them. But Katherine Dunham had spunk and spirit. She fought back.

Katherine Dunham performs a piece from *Star Spangled Rhythm (left)*. Eddie Anderson and Lena Horne act together in *Cabin in the Sky*.

She sued two hotels in Cincinnati and Chicago for refusing to let her stay—and won both cases.  Katherine bristled with anger when she danced in a Kentucky theater where black people had to sit in the balcony.  After the performance, she looked coldly down at the whites in the front rows.  "This is the last time we shall play Louisville," Katherine told them, "because the management refuses to let people like us sit by people like you."

In 1943 with the United States involved in World War II, John was drafted into the army.  Katherine missed him terribly, but she didn't have time to mope.  In addition to her roles as dancer, director, choreographer, and mother hen to a family of spirited young dancers, Katherine had to take over John's job of keeping his costumes and sets in order.  If she had sat down and thought about it, Katherine might have been exhausted.  But with so much to do, who had time for sitting?

As *Tropical Revue* moved from city to city, Katherine continued to experiment with new ideas.  She was forever adding new numbers and changing old ones.  As the popularity of the Dunham Dance Company grew, Katherine's choreography relied more and more on the African ceremonies and dances she had seen in the West Indies.  One new dance, "Rites de Passage" (Rites of Passage), was based on African puberty, fertility, and mating rituals. Both audiences and dance critics loved the dramatic and sensual dance. But according to one critic, it was "nothing to take Grandma to see."

By the time Katherine celebrated her thirty-fifth birthday, she was beginning to slow down a bit as a

Katherine performs *Tropical Revue* with dancer Tommy Gomez.

dancer. Although critics wrote that she was "a stunning performer" and "in the full bloom of her showmanship," arthritis in her knees often left her stiff and sore. But Katherine didn't worry. Arthritis could slow down her dancing but not her creative energy. She devoted more time to choreography. The Dunham Dance Company was made up of talented, professional dancers performing new and exciting dances, and it was wowing audiences like never before.

Katherine Dunham *(far right)* works with her students in a rehearsal.

Despite her success with critics and audiences, Katherine often found herself short of money and struggling to keep her company together.  For some time, the idea of a new dance school had been simmering in her head.  But this school, Katherine decided, would offer more than just dance.  Her work in anthropology had taught her that dance was connected to many other areas of a society's culture.  Katherine wanted to teach dance students about those cultural connections, and she wanted to do it in an atmosphere of racial tolerance.  Above all, she wanted black dance to be treated as a "dignified art."

In 1945 Katherine opened the Katherine Dunham School of Dance in a New York studio donated by Lee Shubert, the famous theater owner.  On the first day of classes, Katherine welcomed 12 students. Ten months later, 420 students bustled in and out of Katherine's classrooms.

Katherine's dance classes focused on some of the movements she had seen during her Caribbean studies. Students learned new techniques, like moving one part of the body while keeping other parts still (a technique known as isolation) and leg extensions without pointed toes. They even learned a snakelike movement of the upper body—the dance of the serpent Damballa. These and other unique dance movements would become known as the "Dunham technique."

Students at Katherine's school could also study tap, ballet, modern, and social dancing. In addition to dance, the school offered classes in drama, speech, philosophy, anthropology, theatrical production, makeup, and several foreign languages. There was so much to choose from that Katherine eventually changed the name of her school to the Katherine Dunham School of Cultural Arts.

More than anything, Katherine was determined that her school would be a haven from the racial prejudice she had lived with all her life. Her classrooms were filled with students of many races, cultures, and backgrounds, children and adults, wealthy and poor. Students who couldn't pay the tuition could earn their lessons by mending costumes or cleaning studios.

Katherine's open mind and big heart earned her love and respect but couldn't pay the bills for her growing school. To help cover expenses, Katherine published *Journey to Accompong,* a book about her visit to Jamaica.

Dancers perform "Shango Dance" *(above)*, choreographed by Katherine Dunham. Dunham strikes a pose in "L'Ag'Ya" *(right)*.

But writing, like dancing, didn't bring in enough money. Katherine padded her modest income any way she could—from choreographing musicals to making records of West Indian music to arranging nightclub acts. Katherine enjoyed her work, but she missed staging her own dance productions. In 1946 the Dunham Dance Company began rehearsals for *Bal Nègre* (Negro Ball), a show that would highlight most of the black dance styles Katherine had learned in her travels.

To add to Katherine's excitement about the new show, the war had ended, and John had come home in time to design the sets and costumes. With Katherine and John teamed up again, *Bal Nègre* was sure to be a success.

Katherine's new production opened on Broadway in November 1946. The show included a new version of "L'Ag'Ya," an exciting snake dance called "Shango Dance," a voodoo ritual dance called "Majumba," and a popular number called "Haitian Roadside." Critics called *Bal Nègre* "far and away the best of the Dunham shows to date."

After the success of *Bal Nègre,* Katherine barely paused long enough to savor the feeling of satisfaction. She was already thinking about what to do next.

Katherine Dunham, wearing a costume and holding a doll from Brazil, gets ready for a performance.

# Return to Paradise

"La Katerina has certainly rung the bell south of the border," reported newspapers about Katherine's trip to Mexico. She has "stolen the heart of London," wrote one British reporter. In Paris, fashionable women flocked to trendy boutiques to buy the latest colorful Dunham line of clothing.

By the time the Dunham Dance Company began its tour through Mexico, South America, and Europe in 1947, Katherine was a celebrity. For the next two years, her life was as colorful as her Caribbean costumes. She and John dined with artists, chatted with actors, and socialized with movie producers from Acapulco to Stockholm. For a small-town girl who had rarely wandered more than hollering distance from home, Katherine had come a long way.

Along with the success of the dance company, however, came plenty of headaches. Gone were the days when Katherine could just choreograph and dance. She had to arrange schedules, negotiate contracts, make travel arrangements, and pack and ship mountains of scenery and costumes. Dancers stayed out too late at night, missed rehearsals, and spent too much money. When a dancer dropped out, Katherine scrambled to find a replacement, calling her school in New York for a student willing to join the company.

In Katherine's absence, enrollment at the school had been dropping. Keeping up with the expenses of the school and supporting her company between performances was a constant challenge. Katherine called it "the old story of great artists—success and financial chaos."

Katherine had always been pretty good at dealing with a dose of hard luck and bad times. But she had started "drinking [alcohol] just about every evening during the show," she admitted years later. She struggled to cope with "a miserable existence, full of discouragement, doubt, anxiety."

In May 1949, things went from bad to worse. Katherine's beloved brother, Albert, died in St. Elizabeth's Hospital in Washington, D.C. She would always refer to his death as "the supreme tragedy" of her life.

After flying home for a brief visit, Katherine returned to the tour. Maybe she hoped that the constant chore of keeping the dance company together would help keep her mind off her troubles. It didn't. Katherine had never felt so down and out. A few months later, Katherine got more bad news. Her father had died.

Katherine Dunham *(by tree)* rehearses with her students in the Boboli Gardens in Florence, Italy.

Just when she needed it most, Katherine got an invitation that perked her up like nothing else could have. The Haitian president Dumarsais Estime asked her to return to Haiti to be entered into the Haitian Legion of Honor for her work, which presented Haiti "in the best light before the rest of the world." The lush jungle of coconut palms, the aroma of oranges and lemons, and the clear blue waters of Haiti gave Katherine the comfort she had longed for. She was home again.

Katherine returned to John and the dance company with a lighter heart and a head full of ideas. Habitation Leclerc was still empty. It was big enough for the whole dance company, she told John. Wouldn't it make wonderful headquarters for the Dunham Dance Company?

Maybe they could buy it someday, she suggested. But until then, why not rent it and take the company to Haiti for a much needed break? John liked the idea.

By the end of 1950, Katherine, John, and a large group of exhausted dancers, musicians, business managers, and secretaries stood on the grounds of Habitation Leclerc. They looked around at the crumbling old mansion, neglected swimming pools, and overgrown gardens. While Katherine and John beamed with pleasure, the others made no attempt to hide their disappointment. This was the paradise Katherine had raved about? The roof leaked and the kitchen stove smoked. Cockroaches swarmed in and out of cracks in the floor, and snakes slept cozily in the mildewed rafters.

Almost immediately, the halls of Habitation Leclerc echoed with grumbles and complaints. When Katherine's widowed stepmother, Annette, arrived for a visit, she added to the air of discontent. What was she supposed to do here in the jungle without television or church meetings?

Katherine hoped that when the dancers went out into the Haitian countryside and saw some authentic African dancing, they would forget about the discomforts of their new home. Surely they would be as inspired by the rituals and dances of Haiti as she had been fifteen years before. To Katherine's disappointment, the dancers weren't interested in watching Haitians dance. They were used to nightclubs and plays, concerts and parties. Haiti bored them.

After four long and unhappy months at Habitation Leclerc, the Dunham Dance Company said good-bye to

Katherine Dunham *(center, holding bag)* and her students arrive home from South America.

Haiti, and Katherine said good-bye to her dream of a permanent island home for the dance company. Once again she watched the shoreline of Haiti fade away and felt as if she were leaving an old friend. She was comforted by the fact that John shared her feelings about Haiti. They both appreciated the beauty of the island and its people—and were willing to tolerate the cockroaches and snakes. The couple agreed to buy Habitation Leclerc and began to make plans to repair and improve it. They would come back to Haiti—someday.

Katherine Dunham with her daughter, Marie-Christine.

During the summer of 1952, while the Dunham Dance Company hopped from city to city in Europe, forty-three-year-old Katherine sometimes found herself feeling old and troubled. Arthritis and age were making performing more difficult. The day-to-day business of touring with the company was wearing her down. It had been a long time since she had had a place to call home. Sometimes she longed to stop moving and stay put. And sometimes she longed for a family.

In December 1952, Katherine and John adopted a French Martinican child, five-year-old Marie-Christine Columbier (who later took the name Dunham-Pratt). Katherine adored her. Until Marie-Christine was old enough to go to school, she traveled with her parents. She loved her life, dressing up in costumes, donning her mother's makeup, and entertaining the dancers with songs from the show. When she reached school age, Katherine and John enrolled her at a boarding school in Switzerland.

By late 1953, the Dunham school was nearing bank-ruptcy. Katherine scrambled to come up with a way to save it. She had a knack for good ideas—but good ideas don't pay bills. In 1954 Katherine had no choice but to close her school. "I feel heartsick," she said.

By the fall of 1955, critics had begun to notice Katherine's physical limitations. Surgery on both knees had helped some, but it was obvious that Katherine wasn't the dancer she used to be. Dance critic Walter Terry wrote that "she rarely indulged in anything more than a hip-swaying shuffle, a mild kick or two."

Katherine performs in "Barrelhouse Shimmy" in 1954.

When the Dunham Dance Company toured Australia, New Zealand, and the Far East in 1956, a cloud of unhappiness loomed over them from the start. Katherine was ill-tempered and demanding. "No one addresses Katherine Dunham as anything but Miss Dunham," reported *People News Magazine,* ". . . not even her husband. His wife, in return, formally addresses him as Mr. P."

"Hard on herself, she is hard on others," noted one New Zealand reporter, "but despite long hours, stormy scenes and low pay . . . the company stays with her."

John was not as tolerant. That fall he left the tour and headed to Haiti. He sent Marie-Christine to stay with relatives in Chicago until he could find a school for her near him.

Katherine's dark mood worsened as the company moved on to the intense heat of Singapore, Hong Kong, and the Philippines. Dancers and stagehands received a daily dose of their boss's sharp tongue and harsh tone.

By the time the tour reached Japan in the summer of 1957, Katherine faced the bitter reality that she simply couldn't continue. She was tired of traveling, tired of the responsibilities of the dance company, and tired of hearing her own angry voice hurt the people she cared about.

On October 4, 1957, after twenty years with the Dunham Dance Company, Katherine called it quits—at least temporarily.

# Finding a New Path

Katherine sat on the rooftop terrace of her rented room in Tokyo, Japan, writing about her childhood. Sometimes the words came spilling out as fast as she could write them. Other times, she gazed out at Mount Fuji and thought hard about what to write about her father, Aunt Lulu, Fanny June Weir, and all the others who had influenced the life of the little girl from Illinois. Half the time she was laughing and half the time she was crying, but one thing was certain. Writing about her life was doing Katherine a lot of good. She wrote to a friend that leaving the dance company and writing her memoirs was "the only way to save the battered remnants of a self that I never actually even knew."

While Katherine was busy writing in Japan, John was in Haiti with Marie-Christine. Without the stress of the dance company, Katherine's ill temper had simmered down, and she and John had begun to patch things up between them. Still thousands of miles away, Katherine stayed in touch with John and Marie-Christine, and planned to reunite with them in Haiti when her writing was done. In the meantime, she faced ever-present money problems. Finally she came up with a way to pay off the taxes she owed, make a decent living, and spend time in Haiti. She and John could turn Habitation Leclerc into a tourist resort! There was only one snag in Katherine's plan. She didn't have the money for the restoration of the run-down estate. Still, she encouraged John to begin the expensive repairs. She hoped her autobiography would bring her the two things she needed badly—peace of mind and the money to fulfill her new dream.

Even though Katherine had been offstage and on her own for nine months, the world hadn't forgotten her. In June 1958, she received an offer to choreograph and direct the dancing scenes in the movie *Green Mansions*. While she was in Hollywood, she found a publisher for her book. Once the filming of *Green Mansions* was complete, Katherine returned to Haiti to put the finishing touches on what she called "the story of the first painful eighteen years of my life." Being with John and Marie-Christine in Haiti worked wonders on Katherine's mood. Calmer and happier than she had been in years, she finished her book. *A Touch of Innocence* was published by Harcourt Brace in the fall of 1959.

Katherine Dunham finishes her autobiography while living in Haiti with John and Marie-Christine.

Katherine loved Haiti throughout her life.

About the same time, Katherine received several honors from the Haitian government, including being named an honorary citizen. Nothing could have pleased her more. Since the first time she had stepped foot on the island twenty-three years before, Katherine had felt that she was "a daughter of Haiti."

The work on Habitation Leclerc was completed in 1961. Katherine and John were pleased with the beautiful grounds, the guest cottages, the Japanese-style bar, and the nightclub decorated with an African theme. Guests at Habitation Leclerc wouldn't be bored. They could visit the small zoo, attend an afternoon tea dance, stroll through the tropical forest, or watch voodoo ritual dances. Katherine and John waited eagerly for tourists to come clamoring to check in. It wasn't long, however, before the hopeful hotel owners realized that Haiti was not the tourist attraction they had hoped it would be. Slums, beggars, disease, and a lack of medical facilities discouraged visitors. In addition, the island was ruled by François Duvalier, the stern dictator nicknamed Papa Doc. His private police force wandered the streets armed with sticks and guns, leaving tourists uneasy and reluctant to stray far from their hotel to enjoy the tropical paradise.

François Duvalier, nicknamed Papa Doc, ruled Haiti in the 1960s.

By the start of 1962, the empty guest cottages at Habitation Leclerc left little doubt that Katherine's plan had failed. As the pile of overdue bills grew taller, she worried about what to do next. When the opportunity to produce a Broadway dance review came up, Katherine and John said yes. Although they would keep Habitation Leclerc so they could return to Haiti, they decided that it was time to go back to what they did best.

That spring, Katherine and John gathered a cast of dancers from villages throughout western Africa, as well as some from the original Dunham Dance Company, and headed for New York to begin rehearsals for their new show. Katherine was excited about dancing and choreographing again. She wanted this production to represent her career in anthropology and her ideas about the evolution of black dance. She named the show *Bamboche* (Haitian for "get-together") and divided it into three parts—a Moroccan dance, a South African dance-drama, and American gospel singing and jazz.

When *Bamboche* opened at the Fifty-fourth Street Theater in New York City on October 22, 1962, Katherine thought it was her best choreography work yet. She also proved she was still a talented dancer. Although fifty-three years old and plagued with arthritis and aching knees, Katherine had as much get-up-and-go as dancers half her age. Reviews of *Bamboche* were good, but the show didn't earn as much money as Katherine and John had hoped. It closed after only a few months.

Katherine kept saying she needed some time "to stop and do some thinking," but when it came to stopping,

Katherine Dunham in *Bamboche*

Katherine Dunham was all talk. When she was asked to choreograph dances for Giuseppe Verdi's opera *Aida*, Katherine said yes. Opera was something new for her, and Katherine enjoyed new challenges.

For *Aida,* which is set in ancient Egypt, Katherine choreographed dances from several African tribal groups. She added some unique touches, like belly dancers and

Moroccan "blue women," women who dyed their skin and clothing dark blue.

Response to the Dunham dance technique in an Italian opera was mixed. Dance critic Walter Terry thought the dances were "dandy for voodoo but not for Verdi." But the performance impressed others, including staff members from Southern Illinois University (SIU) who were looking for someone to stage a production of the opera *Faust*. They thought Katherine was just right for the job. Katherine, of course, agreed. When *Aida* closed, Katherine and John headed for SIU, in Carbondale, Illinois, to begin an eleven-week artist-in-residency program there.

Katherine rehearses with her students for Verdi's opera *Aida*.

Katherine Dunham teaches the Dunham dance technique to a student at Southern Illinois University.

*Faust* tells the story of a man, Dr. Faustus, who sells his soul to the devil, agreeing to spend his afterlife in hell if the devil will give him pleasure and power while on earth. Dr. Faustus reminded Katherine of the German Nazi leader Adolf Hitler. She set her version of *Faust* in World War II Germany. Her dramatic interpretive dances included students playing basketball with a skeleton head, bodies hanging from wires, and the devil roaring across the stage on a motorcycle. *Faust* was presented on the SIU campus on February 13 and 14, 1965. "There was seldom any doubt that the performers were amateurs," reported one reviewer, "but there was also constant proof that the direction was professional."

After the success of *Faust,* the university asked Katherine to continue as a visiting artist in the fine arts department at the SIU campus in Edwardsville, Illinois, about eighty miles from Carbondale.

Katherine gladly accepted the position. One of the first things she did was visit another SIU campus in nearby East St. Louis, Illinois. That visit changed her life. East St. Louis was a troubled community, simmering with racial tension and dragged down by crime and poverty. Garbage piled up on the sidewalks in front of boarded-up buildings. Street gangs roamed the largely black neighborhoods. Children playing in the alleys hardly noticed the sounds of gunshots in the streets nearby. "I was shocked at the violence, the rage so often turned inward on the community," Katherine said after seeing East St. Louis for the first time.

The conditions in East St. Louis got Katherine thinking. Those angry young blacks needed something to do—something to get them off the streets. Katherine decided they needed to dance.

# The Streets of East St. Louis

Katherine had a new dream—to open a school in East St. Louis. Besides dance, she wanted to offer other classes, including foreign languages, percussion, anthropology, and drama. The university thought such a school—a copy of her New York school—would be an important contribution to East St. Louis and wanted to support her efforts. But more funds were needed.

In March 1965, Katherine presented a report to the Office of Economic Opportunity in Washington, D.C., asking for money to establish a school at the university in East St. Louis.

"We can't change the economics of the city, and that of course is the main problem here," Katherine said. "But we can help to give the people an outlook, to show them there is a larger world out there."

Katherine Dunham and President Léopold Senghor discuss the upcoming First World Festival of Negro Arts in Dakar, Senegal.

While she waited for an answer to her request, Katherine taught dance classes, choreographed, and performed. Later that year, she was invited to Senegal, in Africa, to train dancers for the First World Festival of Negro Arts. Katherine and John moved to Dakar, the capital of Senegal, and rented a house with a big front porch. Katherine set up her typewriter and started work on a book about her experiences in Haiti.

Katherine loved Africa and felt the same spiritual connections to the land of her roots as she did to Haiti. To link the two places, she planted herbs from Habitation Leclerc in her garden in Senegal, then later scattered African soil over her yard in Haiti.

Besides making a spiritual connection in Senegal, Katherine made a lifelong friend. Jeanelle Stovall was on vacation from her job as an interpreter for the United Nations in New York. Katherine liked Jeanelle and shared her ideas with her. Jeanelle liked Katherine and her ideas. In 1967 Katherine learned that she had received enough grant money for her school in East St. Louis. Sad to leave Africa but eager to start her new venture, she returned to the United States with John and Jeanelle.

Katherine's new dream had come true. With the support of SIU, she became director of the Performing Arts Training Center. Jeanelle became her assistant for the summer of 1967. After returning to Senegal for a year, she rejoined Katherine's staff in July 1968.

Katherine and John settled into their new home and offices on the SIU campus in Alton, Illinois, a short distance from East St. Louis. Katherine was anxious to plunge into the job of getting the school under way. But she just couldn't stop herself from starting one more project. Besides being a world-class traveler, Katherine was a world-class collector. More than thirty years of travel had left her with an enormous collection of memorabilia, including costumes, musical instruments, pictures, films, and letters. She had never been able to part with a single thing. Storing her treasures had always been a problem.

As the new owner of a large house with lots of room, Katherine decided to open a museum to display her collection. She called it the Dynamic Museum, because everything in her collection could be held or listened to. John agreed to be curator, or director, of the museum.

Katherine and Jeanelle began the slow process of finding students interested in enrolling in the Performing Arts Training Center. Katherine was especially anxious to attract some of the troubled and often violent young people who spent their days and nights hanging out on the streets. "We interviewed in various neighborhood centers where these young people come together," she later recalled, "and immediately we had a following of young militants."

Still, many of the street kids of East St. Louis were suspicious of "a newcomer in town who was interested in them." Katherine needed help convincing them to give her school a chance. As usual, she had an idea. One of the first students to enroll in the Performing Arts Training Center was a young black man named Darryl Braddix. Darryl was a member of a rough street gang called the Imperial War Lords. Katherine asked him to arrange for her to meet with the War Lords. Maybe she could interest them in her school. Darryl agreed.

In July 1967, Katherine, Jeanelle, and Marie-Christine, who was visiting at the time, met with Darryl's gang in a neighborhood tavern. Katherine talked openly and frankly with the wary young men. She told them about the Performing Arts Training Center and described the classes there. When the meeting was over, Darryl and another gang member walked the women back to their car. On the way, the group was confronted by a police officer, who arrested the two men. Katherine demanded to know what the charges were. The police officer answered with a curt "None of your business."

Katherine was furious. She sent Marie-Christine home. Then she and Jeanelle followed the police car to the station, where Katherine continued to demand an explanation for the arrests. Darryl and his friend had the right to an attorney, she told the officers. Realizing that she was being ignored, Katherine planted herself firmly behind the desk. She wasn't moving an inch, she told the surprised police officers, until someone gave her some answers. "One cop started pushing me around and two other big cops started twisting my arms," Katherine later told reporters. "I asked if I were under arrest and they said, 'You sure are!'"

Katherine was arrested for disorderly conduct. Several hours later, John and Marie-Christine arrived to bail her out. Newspapers all over the country reported the details of the story. "Katherine Dunham Is Jailed Three and a Half Hours Following Protest," read the headline in the *New York Times.*

When the East St. Louis police learned that their feisty prisoner was an internationally known choreographer and anthropologist, they dropped the charges. To patch things up, the mayor of East St. Louis presented Katherine with a key to the city, a symbol acknowledging that she would always be welcome there.

When word got around the streets that Katherine Dunham, the woman who opened the Performing Arts Training

Center, had stood up for the Imperial War Lords, some young people decided maybe her school was worth checking out. Gradually, young African Americans drifted off the streets and into the classrooms of the Performing Arts Training Center. Katherine knew that many of those tough kids, especially the men, would be reluctant to try dance classes. She made sure she had classes that would interest them, like judo, karate, and drumming. "They loved to come and drum," Katherine said, "and then they began asking what other courses were being taught." Before long Katherine had many of the young people dancing. Her plan had worked.

One of Katherine's goals with the Performing Arts Training Center was to help the blacks of East St. Louis learn more about their African heritage. "All the young people we came into contact with at that time had a strong wish to become affiliated with Africa," Katherine recalled. "So we offered courses in African drums, and we displayed African sculpture and African-originated dances. It gave them a feeling of identification."

In 1968 Katherine and John moved from Alton to a new home in East St. Louis. "It was too hard for me being so far away from the community where I wanted to work," she said. Katherine and John settled smack-dab in the middle of the slums of East St. Louis. No one was going to say Katherine Dunham was too good for the ghetto. The windows on the first floor of their home on North Tenth Street were boarded up. From the second-floor windows, Katherine and John looked out upon houses with broken windows and burned walls.

Katherine, with some friends from East St. Louis, visits with Senator Adlai Stevenson in Washington, D.C.

Over the next year, the Performing Arts Training Center grew into a well-established branch of SIU. With her friend Jeanelle taking care of the day-to-day business of running the school, Katherine was able to turn her attention back to her book about Haiti. *Island Possessed* was published by Doubleday and Company in 1969. That same year, Katherine organized the Dunham Fund for Research and Development of Cultural Arts to help promote her work.

The Dynamic Museum

In 1970 sixty-one-year-old Katherine was invited to the White House Conference on Children. Katherine proudly took forty-three children from her East St. Louis school to Washington, D.C., to perform karate, percussion, and African dance. "Of course, we stole the show," she said.

While the school continued to thrive, the Dynamic Museum struggled. There wasn't enough room in Katherine's new home to display her large collection and not enough money to pay a staff. Reluctantly, Katherine closed her museum but promised herself she would open it again someday.

Over the next few years, she worked hard to find funding for the museum. With Katherine's reputation and determination, it wasn't hard to find. A group of wealthy supporters called The Friends raised enough money to buy a Victorian mansion on Pennsylvania Avenue in East St. Louis. Once again, Katherine had a home for her treasures. In December 1977, the new Katherine Dunham Dynamic Museum opened to the public. In addition to Katherine's collection of musical instruments and ceremonial costumes, there was a gallery of African and Caribbean art objects collected by both Katherine and Jeanelle during their travels. Katherine was pleased to have her museum in East St. Louis. "I think it's terribly important for both the young and the old people of East St. Louis to be able to come out of their poverty environment and identify with their heritage and see what black cultures in other parts of the world have achieved," Katherine said. "Hopefully, the careful selection of the pieces and their tasteful arrangement will make the people of East St. Louis feel less isolated and will, perhaps more than anything else we've been doing here, give them a real feeling of hope. Beauty rubs off, you know."

In the following years, Katherine received recognitions of her contribution to dance, including the NAACP Lifetime Achievement Award and the Presidential Medal of Arts. As other ethnic and black dance companies formed, such as the Dance Theatre of Harlem and the Alvin Ailey American Dance Theater, Katherine got credit for paving the way. Critic Arthur Todd wrote that she "put serious Negro dancing on the map once and for all."

Coretta Scott King *(left)*, Melba Moore *(center)*, and Katherine Dunham *(right)* receive an award in 1987.

In January 1979, Katherine received the Albert Schweitzer Music Award "for a life dedicated to music and devoted to humanity." At the award ceremony at Carnegie Hall in New York, dancers from Katherine's school and former members of the Dunham Dance Company presented a program of dances representing Katherine's long career, including "Rites de Passage" and "Shango Dance."

In 1982, fifteen years after she had opened the doors of the Performing Arts Training Center, Katherine retired from her position at the university. But the seventy-three-year-old anthropologist, choreographer, and teacher had no intention of cutting her ties with the cultural community of East St. Louis. With Jeanelle's help, Katherine turned her attention to the Dunham Fund for Research and Development of Cultural Arts, which would later be renamed the Katherine Dunham Centers for the Arts and Humanities. The centers were established to provide year-round dance training for children and seminars in Dunham technique as well as to support the Dynamic Museum.

In 1986 John Pratt died. Katherine missed her husband and partner terribly. On her own, she maintained her ties to Haiti. She often rented suites at Habitation Leclerc to friends and fellow artists. She had a thatch-roofed hut built there where she could continue her voodoo studies. She hoped to become a voodoo priestess, like her old friends Téoline and Dégrasse.

In 1992 eighty-two-year-old Katherine made headlines by fasting (not eating) to protest the U.S. government turning away Haitians who were trying to escape violent political struggles in their homeland. Her daughter, Marie-Christine, a Dunham dance teacher in Rome, Italy, came to East St. Louis to be with her mother during the fast. After forty-seven days, Katherine ended her fast at the urging of deposed Haitian president Jean-Bertrand

A Haitian refugee in the Haitian camp at the United States military base in Guantánamo Bay, Cuba, asks for asylum. Like many Haitians, he is trying to escape the political turmoil in Haiti.

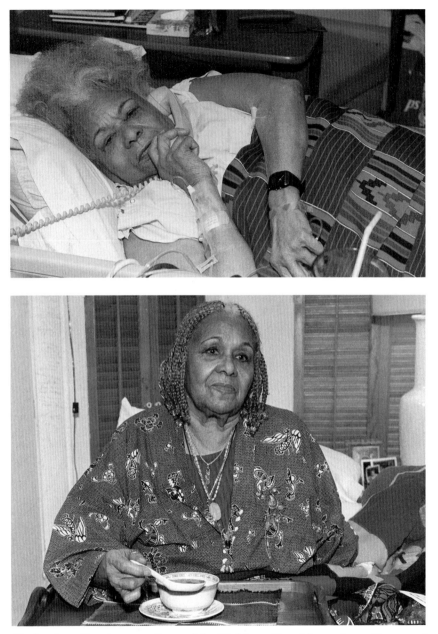

Katherine Dunham talks with Haitian President Jean-Bertrand Aristide by phone during her fast in 1992 *(top)*. Katherine ends her fast with a bowl of soup on March 18, 1992 *(above)*.

Aristide. Katherine had shown her commitment to the people of Haiti and had helped to bring their plight to the attention of many Americans.

Katherine Dunham has spent her life exploring the roots of black dance and appreciating the wide range of cultures throughout the world. Above all, however, she believes in the worth and dignity of all, regardless of race. When asked about her philosophy of life, Katherine once said, "I am a firm believer in what human beings can do." Katherine's faith in herself—and faith in others—has never died. Asked at one time what she would like to see written on her tombstone, she replied, "She tried."

# About the Katherine Dunham Centers for the Arts and Humanities

The Katherine Dunham Centers for the Arts and Humanities were established to preserve Katherine Dunham's contribution to dance and anthropology. Another purpose is to provide training in the arts for the young people of East St. Louis, Illinois. Over the years, the Dunham Centers have attracted dancers, choreographers, artists, educators, and researchers from all over the world.

In addition to conducting workshops and seminars, the centers operate the Katherine Dunham Dynamic Museum. A historic two-story building in the Pennsylvania Avenue Historic District holds things that Katherine collected during her travels. The museum is the only cultural center in East St. Louis.

The first floor holds many of Katherine's artworks and musical instruments. In the Haitian Room, visitors can view paintings, furniture, carvings, macramé (items made of knotted cord), and other art relics from African and Caribbean cultures. The Dynamic Room displays West African sculpture, masks, and tapestries. The Music Room contains Katherine's collection of percussion instruments from all over the world. Photographs of some of these objects are shown on the centers' website at www.imlab.uiuc.edu/eslarp/ntac/Dunham.htm.

Participants in a children's workshop at the Katherine Dunham Centers dance for a 1988 television production.

The museum's second floor is devoted to Katherine's career as a dancer, choreographer, anthropologist, writer, and teacher. Museum visitors can see some of her original costumes and headdresses. People can browse through scrapbooks, photographs, and letters. Some of the fashion and set designs of Katherine's late husband, John Pratt, are also on display.

The Katherine Dunham Centers for the Arts and Humanities remain a vital cultural center. They preserve Katherine Dunham's legacy and fulfill her dream of showing the people of East St. Louis that "there is a larger world out there."

In the early 1920s, Katherine excelled as a student dancer at the University of Chicago.

# Bibliography

**Books:**

Beckford, Ruth. *Katherine Dunham: A Biography.* New York: Marcel Dekker, 1979.

Dominy, Jeanine. *Katherine Dunham.* New York: Chelsea House, 1992.

Dunham, Katherine. *Dances of Haiti.* Los Angeles: Center for Afro-American Studies, University of California, 1983.

Dunham, Katherine. *Island Possessed.* U. of Chicago, 1969.

Dunham, Katherine. *A Touch of Innocence.* New York: Harcourt, Brace, 1959.

Harnan, Terry. *African Rhythm—American Dance: A Biography of Katherine Dunham.* New York: Knopf, 1974.

Haskins, James. *Black Dance in America: A History through Its People.* New York: Thomas Y. Crowell, 1990.

Haskins, James. *Katherine Dunham.* New York: Coward, McCann & Geoghegan, 1981.

Haskins, James. *Voodoo and Hoodoo: Their Tradition and Craft as Revealed by Actual Practitioners.* New York: Stein and Day, 1978.


**Articles:**

"Dunham Continues Her Fast in Support of Haitians." *Jet Magazine,* volume 81, issue 20 (March 9, 1992).

Gleick, Elizabeth, Nina Burleigh, and Mary Harrison. "Hunger Strike." *People Weekly,* volume 37, issue 12 (March 30, 1992).

"This Week in Black History." *Jet Magazine,* volume 87, issue 3 (November 21, 1994).

# Index

AAW - 8426